Decision Making 101

Know for Sure

■ ■ ■

By Prince Handley

University of Excellence Press

Copyright © 2012 by Prince Handley
All Rights Reserved.

UNIVERSITY OF EXCELLENCE PRESS
Los Angeles ◼ London ◼ Tel Aviv

ISBN-13: 978-0692356128
ISBN-10: 0692356126

Printed in the USA

First Edition

The only Guidance book you need!

TABLE OF CONTENTS

FOREWORD

The message in this book is extremely important for you—not only for your personal life, but also for economic decisions—and for your future.

Life is full of options. Sometimes you need to make decisions with "the facts in hand." Things are pretty clear-cut. It is just a matter of which option is better for you. However, **there are times when you have to make a decision that is more subjective**—and one that is critical.

There are, and will be, many things—stressful things—which will push and pull on you from different spheres. **Do NOT be "tricked" into making a bad decision**.

No matter how successful you are ... you **could** still make a bad decision. I want to help protect you so that you can live a peaceful, happy and productive life. What you are learning in this book has cost me dearly in terms of money, confusion and time.

It is my prayer that you will learn from it—**put it into practice**—and NOT suffer consequences keeping you from advancement in INCREASE and GREATNESS for yourself and for others ... and especially for the LORD.

Say "Goodbye" to frustration and confusion. From now on you can **"Know for Sure!"** You will want to use this book, also, as **a guide for global economic shifts** in the uncertain waters ahead.

Decision Making 101

Know for Sure

■ ■ ■

● ADVANCE ONLY WHEN YOU ARE SURE

I am going to cover extensively HOW to KNOW when God is leading you into new territory—new endeavor—and when it is NOT God leading you. Remember ... you have an enemy!

And no matter how long you have known and served God, you can **still** make mistakes if you're not careful. By that I mean ... there is a possibility of you making a wrong decision that could affect your future well being.

In this book you will learn every aspect of decision making, and more importantly: HOW to follow your heart. And if you don't need this message now—believe me—you will sometime in the future.

QUESTION

➡ Do you have peace NOW because **you backed away from advancement** in fear, unbelief or mental anxiety from the position or territory where the LORD wanted you to advance, and the devil is NOT bothering you about it (resisting you) anymore?

OR ...

➡ You are in the will of God, and you are experiencing God's peace because **you obeyed** and went forward?

Spiritual warfare is a "double edged" sword. We usually think of it as offensive—that is, on our part—resisting, opposing and doing battle in prayer and with the Holy Spirit against Satan and his forces.

Often, what we do NOT contemplate, or weigh pragmatically—as far as real time strategy to be analyzed—is that **the enemy has a specific strategy** of opposition in plan against our advancement(s) and increase ... and especially for NEW frontier work.

We know the devil has devices he wants to use in opposition to our increase and greatness for ourselves, but especially for God's Kingdom. However, even though we bind and loose, pray and resist, **we fail many times to obtain the specifics of military tactics in use by the enemy**.

This is where three (3) of the Gifts of the Holy Spirit come into play:

- The Word of Knowledge;

- The Word of Wisdom; and,

- The Gift of Discernment.

Yet, even though we know what these gifts are and how they operate, it does NOT mean that by the knowledge of the same that we are receiving true, specific and accurate intelligence (military intel) about the enemy's detailed plans—and, objectives—to restrain or contain us. I am NOT saying it is the fault of the Gifts, but that **it is our fault for NOT being masters of the weaponry we have available**.

Knowing HOW to administer CPR is different than being SKILLFUL in administering the same effectively.

Let me say this unequivocally, and at the same time ... encourage and challenge you: your job is to win and to have peace continuously!

YOUR JOB IS TO WIN AND TO HAVE PEACE CONTINUOUSLY

PROTECT YOURSELF FROM CONFUSION

When you are confused, it is NOT God's fault. It is either YOUR fault or the devil's fault. And when you boil it down, it is simply YOUR fault for allowing the enemy to do this to you. The purpose of this writing is NOT to condemn you, but rather to enlighten you to the fact that you CAN and SHOULD have peace continuously in your life. There are many verses on peace in the Holy Bible.

■ Isaiah 26:3 *"You will keep him in perfect **peace**, whose mind is fixed on You, because he trusts in You."*

■ John 14:27 *"Peace I leave with you, my **peace** I give unto you: not as the world gives, give I unto you. Let not your heart be troubled, neither let it be afraid."* – Jesus

■ Philippians 4:6-7 *"Be in anxiety about nothing; but in everything by prayer and supplication with thanksgiving let your requests be made known unto God. And the **peace** of God, which passes all understanding, shall guard your hearts and minds through Messiah Jesus."*

Let me present **a major KEY to the reason for the confusion and lack of peace** in many of YOUR plans, strategies, and advancement attempts for increase and greatness. The major key is not negative thinking (although that's one source); it is not self-deprecation (although that can be a reason). But a major KEY is: **You did not pray through at the start (before you initiated the advancement) until you had assurance —YOU WERE NOT SURE—as to whether the LORD wanted you to do what you were attempting to do.**

9

If you really KNOW God wants you to do something, then there is NO confusion that cannot be dealt with effectively with faith, the Word of God and prayer.

You can start a project, initiate a new business endeavor or ministry outreach, and when it is starting to form you can get confused: **it scares the enemy even IF you weren't supposed to do it**. And, it scares the enemy even more IF you were supposed to do it. However, **IF you KNOW it is of God, then you will have confidence to proceed** no matter what or who comes against you.

Isaiah 30:21 is a KEY verse concerning opposition and confusion of and by the enemy ... and this same verse is a KEY verse concerning the leading of the LORD. *"Your ears shall hear a word behind you, saying, 'This is the way, you walk in it.' When you turn to the right hand and when you turn to the left."*

It is so imperative that you understand this because many of God's people—even some of His servants— have committed suicide because **they were so oppressed mentally due to continuing in a path of confusion toward a good objective, but one they were NOT supposed to be pursuing.**

Your mistake in this type of situation is that you were NOT supposed to be doing what you are, or were, doing in the first place!

Just because it is good or productive—or even helps advance the Kingdom—does NOT mean it is, or was, what God wants you to be doing at this time in your life.

EXAMPLE

You might have even started out to do it before but then hesitated—NOT SURE—and then ceased the advancement. Then, you started again (after convincing yourself). Possibly, you were subtly "influenced" to initiate this advancement due to the needs of others and the increase of what it would bring to both you and them.

FOLLOW YOUR HEART

If you are walking with God and living for Him, you can follow your heart: **the Holy Spirit will lead you in your inner man**. You will be able to tell—or, to know—when things are "off", or not "quite right."

Lots of people—even God's People—have travelled deeper into confusion because they continued on in a path they should NOT be traveling. I'm not talking about a path of sin, rebellion or ungodliness. It might be a path of good and productive effort with the goal in mind of contributing to the Kingdom of the Lord. However, not all paths are yours or mine to take.

You may have already spent time and money initiating the process in which you are involved—or, the path which you are traveling. **CAUTION**: If you feel NOW that you should NOT be doing this, then get off the path—TURN AROUND—go back to where you had peace before: **even if it costs you!**

We read an interesting experience that happened in the life of Amaziah, the king of Judah (the portion of Scripture in 2 Chronicles 25:5-9). He had gathered 300,000 men from Judah to go to war, plus another 100,000 from Israel for 100 talents of silver.

> *"But there came a man of God to him, saying, O king, don't let the army of Israel go with you, for the LORD is not with Israel, with all the children of Ephraim.*
>
> *But if you will go, do valiantly, and be strong for the battle: God will cast you down before the*

enemy; for God has power to help, and to cast down.

*Amaziah said to the man of God, **'But what shall we do for the hundred talents which I have given to the army of Israel?'** The man of God answered, **'The LORD is able to give you much more than this.'"***

King Amaziah obeyed the man of God—*he turned his back on the money he had already invested to hire the Israeli military forces*—and experienced victory.

If you are wondering if you are being "double minded," you need to make sure of this decision. Conversely, this is **EXACTLY WHY** you should have made sure of the decision before you initiated the advancement. (We will cover more on this later in the book.)

Our beloved Jewish brother, Ya'akov, says:

"If any of you lack wisdom, let him ask of God, who gives to all men with an open hand, and without an unkind word, and it shall be given to him."

But let him ask in faith, nothing wavering. *For he that wavers is like a wave of the sea driven with the wind and tossed.*

For let not that man think that he shall receive any thing of the Lord.

A double minded man is unstable in all his ways."

– Brit Chadashah: James 1:5-8

At this point you may think you are unstable by being "double minded." Well, ask yourself this question: *"Am I better off continuing in this endeavor if I do NOT have peace about it—or am I better off to turn back to the place where I had peace before."*

THIS BRINGS TO THE FRONT A SITUATION FOR WHICH YOU MUST HAVE DISCERNMENT

Is it the devil trying to discourage you through doubt? **Is the devil afraid of the great rewards** that will be reaped by your continuing on in the advancement that you have initiated?

14

OR ...

Did you make a mistake by initiating an advancement that you were to start at another time (at a later date, but not now)?

ANSWER

After praying, **what do you have peace about doing?** Continuing on? **...** Or, turning around?

Let's look at Isaiah 30:21 again. We read a beautiful record of the leading of God.

"Your ears shall hear a word behind you, saying, 'This is the way, you walk in it, when you turn to the right hand, and when you turn to the left."

Learn to listen to the voice of the LORD: *"This is the way; you walk in this direction."*

NOTICE: I had to do this one time. It not only cost me lots of money that **I would have made**, but **it also cost me lots of money to turn around.**

Another thing to consider is that maybe your body—or, your mind—is telling you to turn around. There may be a physiological problem that could occur up the road, and God is trying to warn you ahead of time.

The psychosomatic and neurological complexes of your mind and body influence each other: but—unknown to many—**they also help monitor your physiological processes** in a way which can be helpful. God can speak to you through them if you listen. This does NOT contradict divine healing, or the fact that there is healing in The Atonement purchased by the BLOOD of Mashiach Yeshua (Messiah Jesus). But, just like the auto mechanic can repair cars, a clanking piston may be an indication of a broken piston rod that needs repair.

IF YOU'RE NOT SURE ... DON'T

This is WHY you have to **MAKE SURE at the beginning**—BEFORE YOU START—that you WANT TO—you're supposed to—do this thing. You need to KNOW that you are to initiate, carry forward and FINISH the proposed advancement.

This way, when confusion or doubt enters in, you will be able—**you will want to**—resist confusion in faith and with confidence and continue the advancement.

16

*"Now faith is **assurance** of things hoped for, proof of things not seen. For by this the elders obtained testimony of a good report."* – Brit Chadashah Hebrews 11:1 (New Testament)

*"And the work of righteousness shall be peace; and the effect of righteousness quietness and **assurance** forever."* – Tanakh: Isaiah 32:17 (Hebrew Scriptures)

*"Let us draw near with a true heart in full **assurance** of faith, having our hearts sprinkled from an evil conscience, and our bodies washed with pure water."* – Brit Chadashah: Hebrews 10:22 (New Testament)

When you **know for sure** you are on the divinely inspired route for a particular advancement, whenever doubt or unbelief or fear arise to challenge you, remember to simply **claim and do** the following:

"Be in anxiety about nothing; but in everything by prayer and supplication with thanksgiving let your requests be made known unto God. And the peace of God, which passes all understanding, shall guard your hearts and minds through Messiah Jesus."

In this petition you can ask God:

17

- To help you;

- To give you wisdom if you do NOT know how to operate in the advancement; and,

- To encourage you all the way to victory

➡ Remember to THANK HIM during your request because you KNOW He is going to answer you! Then ... God's peace will guard your heart and mind: **it will be your sentry to protect you.** When God sees you thanking Him ahead of time He knows you are believing, and He adds it to your faith account.

We are living in an age which is very volatile spiritually. The People of God—true believers—are making great advancements in and for the Kingdom through divine intelligence and strategy. This is WHY the enemy is so frustrated and wants to unleash vigorous attacks upon your mind and effort.

REMEMBER: The victory has already been purchased by our Leader, Messiah Yeshua. **It is finished.** You have been given the KEYS to Heaven and Hell: the KEYS of binding and loosing. Just make sure that the advancements you propose are **for sure** according to the Will of God before you start them. The Holy Spirit will lead you in your inner man—your human spirit—and **you will know for sure**.

● BINDING AND LOOSING

A few years ago the LORD started speaking to me about **"Binding and Loosing."** Although I knew the basic precepts of "Binding and Loosing" and had used those scriptural principles for years in situations dealing with spiritual authority, the LORD impressed me to be more active and militant in the use of them.

Let's first look into what the scripture says concerning this teaching of Jesus. After the Apostle Peter declared to Yeshua (Jesus), *"You are the Messiah, the Son of the living God,"* the Lord **gave him KEYS as to how he would build His Kingdom**. He told Shimon (Peter):

"And I will give unto you the keys of the kingdom of heaven: and whatever you bind on earth will be bound in heaven: and whatever you loose on earth will be loosed in heaven." – Mattiyahu (Matthew) 16:19

A little while later—in teaching about dealing with problems in interpersonal relationships—Jesus said:

19

"Assuredly I say unto you, Whatever you bind on earth will be bound in heaven: and whatever you loose on earth will be loosed in heaven." – Mathew 18:18

Interestingly enough, **if we examine this passage in the original language** – *[See Textual Notes at back of this book for language info.]* Jesus probably spoke Hebrew in both of these passages as He was teaching His talmidim (disciples) and they were ALL Jewish, but the text was later recorded into Koine Greek (the lingua franca of the day) – **we see an amazing truth**. In the original we are reading literally: "Whatever you bind (or loose) on earth **shall already have been** bound (or loosed) in heaven." **The verb form reflects action that has been achieved in the past has now become active in the present**. The past action refers to **Messiah's complete triumph** on the cross-stake.

Now that we have discussed this important truth, let me share how God dealt with me. Shortly after the LORD began speaking to me to be more active and militant in "binding and loosing" I was flying to Cincinnati (USA) to teach at a seminar and miracle meeting. A Baptist pastor picked me up at the airport and on the way to the church we had to put the automobile on a ferry, or

20

barge, to cross a river. The pastor and I were outside the car on the boat ferry and he began to tell me an amazing thing.

He told me, **"God has been dealing with me about 'binding and loosing.'"** I had NOT told him that the LORD had been dealing with me about the same thing. It was a blessed seminar with the presence of the Holy Spirit. However, I soon forgot about what the pastor had told me.

Later I was in Africa for about one month and the LORD worked mighty in MIRACLES and healings and salvation ... opening doors for me to minister in many public schools. The gifts of the Spirit operated wonderfully and students were healed and saved.

The day I returned home from Africa, I received a message from a pastor who asked me to come to his home and minister to a young minister. He told me the minister had a mighty youth ministry but was discouraged because of people in the "false covering" movement trying to hold him back and control him. I said to my friend, "I just returned from Africa and need to rest. I will not come now, but if the LORD leads me to come minister to the young man I will call you."

About 3 days later (which was the last day the young man would be in town ... he lived about 1,800 miles / 2900 km away), God told me to go visit him. I called my friend and told him and he invited me to dinner that evening. During my visit, the LORD gave me a prophecy for the young man. I told him, **"Go back and start a church!"** That church now has different campuses in two different states and I think over 10,000 members.

While visiting at the pastor's house, before I left, he told me, "There are some people you need to meet." Again, I mentioned that I needed some rest; however, the LORD told me: **"Meet these people."** I invited the people to my home, and what a blessing it was. There last name was Morse, and one of them had written a book titled, *Exodus to a Hidden Valley,* by Eugene Morse. (There is also a *Reader's Digest* account of their ministry; however, it is "toned down" as they had to work in collaboration with the publishers.)

There were three generations of them visiting me: grandfather, father and son. The family (from oldest to youngest) had **ministered in Burma (Indo-China) for 51 years** (from oldest to youngest) and had been

imprisoned by the Communists three times. There was lots of demonization and false religion in that area in Southeast Asia: the majority practicing Theravada-Buddhism with some of the tribal people practicing animism and shamanism.

The Morse's told me that they had labored almost **without** fruit—without people coming to Christ—for years. Then, the LORD told them to **"bind" Satan and cast him out of the areas where they would be ministering**. Immediately they started seeing people come to Christ. Then, the LORD instructed them to **"loose" the Holy Spirit" into the areas where they would be ministering**. After that, a great harvest of souls—people receiving Christ—resulted. As I remember around 65,000 people received the LORD and many were baptized in water. They labored for the LORD among the Lisu tribe and helped in the migration —the escape—of 1,000's of Christians into and through the jungle.

▦ THE KEY ▦

God is waiting upon you to do the "binding and loosing." **He wants YOU to do your part and work with Him in intercession**. When you do your part—

binding and loosing—then the finished work of Messiah Jesus takes effect ... and what you have bound or loosed ... will **already** have been bound or loosed in Heaven!

▦ WILL YOU DO IT? ▦

So, my challenge to you is this: **Take advantage of "binding and loosing."** This principle works in your personal life, your family, your ambitions, your business and for service for the LORD. Your leader, Jesus the Messiah, taught this. And remember, *"Whatever you bind (or loose) on earth* **shall already have been** *bound (or loosed) in heaven."* Listen to God ... and NOT men!

What is that GREAT thing you want to do in your personal life, your family, your business or for God? What is the deep stirring in your heart for service unto the LORD? Nations and unreached tribal groups are hanging in the balance: waiting for you to be the one who reaches them—or, who coordinates projects to reach them—in these Last Days. Remember, **Just MAKE SURE God is leading you to do it.**

● WHAT TO DO WITH BAD DECISIONS

If you are walking with God and living for Him, you can follow your heart: the inner man will lead you. You will be able to tell—or, to know—when things are "off", or not "quite right."

If you're NOT sure, then don't!

Do NOT make rash decisions.

This is one of the greatest lessons I have learned in life.

- Stay in the "peace" zone

- Making rash decisions can bind you

In this section of the book **I will tell you HOW to be delivered from any situation**—in case you have made, or will make, a wrong decision. There are certain steps you can take to obtain freedom and peace again.

When you feel pressured to do something—if you do NOT have peace about it—WAIT—do NOT go forward. It is better to be at peace—to stay in the "peace zone" than to go ahead—even if it looks good!

This—the pressure—can be a trick of the enemy to get you in bondage and mental duress. Pray about the situation. Do NOT let people—even friends—coerce you or persuade you to take action IF you do not have peace about the situation.

I promised God one time that I would never do anything—or take action concerning anything—that I was NOT sure about. If I had a question about the situation, or if I did NOT have peace, I promised God that I would NOT go forward. The reason I made this promise to God was that I got into a very difficult and emotionally trying situation as a result of a speedy—a rash—decision.

Lots of times people are **emotionally distressed** because of such uncertain behavior: **going ahead of God!** Although not the majority of cases, sometimes the enemy of your soul can **wound you emotionally as a result of a bad decision**, especially IF it is a decision involving another person. As a matter of fact, the whole reason for confusion in the matter can many times be traced to some deception concocted by the enemy to force you to make a bad decision—a hurried decision—one you were NOT sure about making in the first place. In case you are feeling **emotionally distressed as a result of a bad decision**, read my book: *Healing of Emotional Wounds*. It will help you.

NOTHING CAN BIND YOU IF YOU WILL LISTEN TO GOD & FOLLOW YOUR HEART

HOW TO END FRUSTRATION

When frustration is invading you, back up one step— **analyze the situation.** Analyze WHO and WHAT is blocking you—keeping you at a "dead end." Get up and do something about it. It may be YOU that is blocking you. Some people are their own greatest enemies. The problem is always "someone else." They have a "dead-end" mindset. If you're driving your automobile and find yourself at a dead end, that doesn't mean YOU are at a dead end! **GET OUT AND WALK.**

When you are frustrated, many times you are sick; maybe not physically, but emotionally, spiritually or financially. And the real reason you are sick and frustrated is because you are NOT trusting God. You may even feel sick in your human spirit (your heart)— you feel "lean" in your soul—because you're leaning on or trusting someone else **other than God**.

If you are leaning on someone other than God to take care of and provide for you, then do NOT expect God to lead you!

I am going to tell you WHAT to do **if you are bound and have lost peace**—that is, you have become emotionally disturbed—**as the result of going ahead of God.**

■ **First**, PROMISE God that you will **NEVER do anything again unless you have peace about it.** That is, you will make NO rash decisions. God loves you, my friend, and He does NOT want you bound by unwise decisions and actions. He paid the GREATEST price—the gift of His Son, Messiah Jesus, so that you can be FREE!

■ **Second**, ASK God to **turn the situation around** and

smite Satan through it, and give you a BLESSING in spite of what you have done. Ask God for mercy. Read the Book of Micah, Chapter Seven, verses 7 thru 10 in the the Tanakh (the Hebrew Scriptures, or Old Testament.)

▪ **Third**, give a GIFT to God. As a result of God turning the situation around, and for His mercy and kindness in restoring you, **promise God ahead of time** that you will give Him a certain specific gift—or that you will take a certain specific action of love and/or sacrifice—as a gift of thanksgiving to Him for providing your MIRACLE. You can give the gift to God either before or after your answer.

▪ **Fourth, THANK God ahead of time ... and every day ... for His deliverance that He is going to show you**. He WILL show Himself strong in your behalf IF YOU are sincere.

I learned the SECRET I have shared with you the HARD WAY. And through the years, I have seen the manifold mercies of God as a result of what He taught me—even through my RASH decisions—even decisions that looked good, or that other people thought were good, but that I did NOT have peace about when I made them.

For some short lessons in areas of every day—common sense—life, listen to my "mini" podcasts at: princehandley.libsyn.com. You can also purchase an APP to receive them on your iPhone, tablet or other device through Apple.com

---

Yes, **stay in "the zone"** where you will experience continual freedom: **the "peace zone."**

Once there, stay there ... don't let anyone or anything get you out of the zone.

And—if you need some help with direction—here are some scriptures for you:

- Psalm 27:11
- Jeremiah 42:3
- I Kings 19:9-12
- Isaiah 30:21

● SUMMARY AND REVIEW

Realize that there are times when God may not only show you **for sure** what to do, but **He may also give you detailed, specific plans of what to do**. One example of this is in the life of King David, where God revealed to David exact plans of building the Temple.

"All this, said David, the LORD made me understand in writing by his hand upon me, even all the works of this pattern." – 1 Chronicles 28:19

Finally, one reason I have written this book is not only to help you in family, personal or spiritual decisions, but also because of the current economy and the forthcoming stress forces that will operate in the future. Europe is in GREAT trouble economically; however, the USA eventually will suffer GREATER hardship.

Since we are now a global economy acted upon by an international financial complex, what happens in one sector influences the whole spectral range. But since the US Dollar is still—at this time—the leading support for world currency, **when the US falls, the world economy will also take a more devastating plunge**.

So, no matter what country you live in, the advice in this book applies to you economically as well.

Psalm 37:3 tells us: *"Trust in the LORD, and do good; so shall you dwell in the land, and truly you shall be fed."*

I want to "stretch" your mind to force you to think—to re-evaluate—current or future decisions because of the current economy and the forthcoming stress forces that will operate in the future; i.e., **situations in unfamiliar grounds**.

In Habbakuk 2:4 (Tanakh) we read: *"Behold, his soul which is lifted up is not upright in him: but the just shall live by his faith."* **Be careful of pride: it will bring you down**. And, in the future economy you for sure don't want to be "brought down." The GREAT NEWS is that "Those who have been made in right standing with God by the sacrifice of Mashiach Yeshua, Son of David, will be restored and live—AND continue in wholeness—by their faith and moral integrity." **GO FORWARD!**

TEXTUAL NOTES

1. Hebrew was regarded as *Lashon Ha-Kodesh,* the sacred language of the Jewish people. Independent linguistic evidence indicates that Hebrew was used as a common language during the late second Temple period. For example, J.T. Milik wrote, "Mishnaic [Hebrew] … was at that time the spoken dialect of the inhabitants of Judaea" *(Ten Years of Discovery in the Wilderness of Judaea).*

2. Koine is the Greek word for "common." Koine Greek (also called New Testament Greek) was the form of the Greek language used from around 300 BC to AD 300.

⸸

"Call to me and I will answer you, and show you great and mighty things which you do not know."
– Tanakh: Jeremiah 33:3

LIVE A LIFE OF EXCELLENCE!

UNIVERSITY OF EXCELLENCE PRESS
Los Angeles ▪ London ▪ Tel Aviv

NOTE

We listen to our readers. Tell us what **new** subject matter you would like to see published. Email your ideas to: universityofexcellence@gmail.com.

See following pages for Bonus & Announcement

BONUS

To help you, and to help you teach others, we have prepared Rabbinical Studies at this site:

www.uofe.org/RABBINICAL_STUDIES.html

These are commentaries from **ancient** Jewish Rabbis that identify the Mashiach of Israel.

To help you, and to help you teach others, we have also prepared Bible Studies in English, Spanish and French.

- English FREE Bible Studies
   www.uofe.org/english_bible_studies.html

- Spanish FREE Bible Studies
   www.uofe.org/spanish_bible_studies.html

- French FREE Bible Studies
   www.uofe.org/french_bible_studies.html

ANNOUNCEMENT

We recommend you obtain the following book in case you have experienced emotional wound as a result of a bad or unwise decision: *Healing of Emotional Wounds.*

Make sure you study the following companion books to this book in the **Success Series** by Prince Handley:

Action Keys for Success

How to Do Great Works

Success Cycles and Secrets

Victory Over Opposition and Resistance

Resurrection Multiplication – Miracle Production

All the above books are available at Amazon and other book stores. See the last page for complete book list. Go here for book updates > marketplaceworld.com

⁜

For seminars with Prince Handley, contact:

universityofexcellence@gmail.com

OTHER BOOKS BY PRINCE HANDLEY

- Map of the End Times
- How to Do Great Works
- Flow Chart of Revelation
- Action Keys for Success
- Health and Healing Complete Guide to Wholeness
- Prophetic Calendar for Israel & the Nations: Thru 2023
- Healing Deliverance
- How to Receive God's Power with Gifts of the Spirit
- Healing for Mental and Physical Abuse
- Victory Over Opposition and Resistance
- Healing of Emotional Wounds
- How to Be Healed and Live in Divine Health
- Healing from Fear, Shame and Anger
- How to Receive Healing and Bring Healing to Others
- New Global Strategy: Enabling Missions
- The Art of Christian Warfare
- Success Cycles and Secrets
- New Testament Bible Studies (A Study Manual)
- Babylon the Bitch – Enemy of Israel
- Resurrection Multiplication – Miracle Production
- Faith and Quantum Physics – Your Future
- Conflict Healing – Relational Health
- Decision Making 101 – Know for Sure
- Total Person Toolbox
- Prophecy, Transition & Miracles

AVAILABLE AT AMAZON AND OTHER BOOK STORES
UNIVERSITY OF EXCELLENCE PRESS
Los Angeles ■ London ■ Tel Aviv

www.ingramcontent.com/pod-product-compliance
Lightning Source LLC
Chambersburg PA
CBHW060645030426

42337CB00018B/3463